C.S.
Illustrations b

A White-Tailed John Called Moose
(and 19 other silly-ish poems)

Bumblebee Books
London

BUMBLEBEE PAPERBACK EDITION

Copyright © C.S. Wiezak 2023
Illustrations by Rosie McAdam

The right of C.S. Wiezak to be identified as author of
this work has been asserted in accordance with sections 77 and 78 of the
Copyright, Designs and Patents Act 1988.

All Rights Reserved

No reproduction, copy or transmission of this publication
may be made without written permission.
No paragraph of this publication may be reproduced,
copied or transmitted save with the written permission of the publisher, or
in accordance with the provisions
of the Copyright Act 1956 (as amended).

Any person who commits any unauthorised act in relation to
this publication may be liable to criminal
prosecution and civil claims for damage.

A CIP catalogue record for this title is
available from the British Library.

ISBN: 978-1-83934-039-0

Bumblebee Books is an imprint of
Olympia Publishers.

First Published in 2023

Bumblebee Books
Tallis House
2 Tallis Street
London
EC4Y 0AB

Printed in Great Britain

www.olympiapublishers.com

Dedication

To Jessica and May

Contents

Animal House 7

Seasoned 11

Gordon 12

Worm 14

Traffic Jam 15

Clothes 16

Insects & Tadpole 18

Dinner with a Stork 20

Henry the Shark 22

Mr Snips 24

Dreams 26

Vegetable Prison 27

A White Tailed John Called Moose 31

Chips 34

Eight Hands 36

Yummy 38

Animal Noises 40

Frog 42

Animal Olympics 44

Girl with a Moustache 46

Animal House

The old man had been working hard,
So he went upstairs for a bath.
But after a few turns of the tap,
Out popped the head of a giraffe.

'What on earth?' said the man,
'This is quite preposterous!'
He tried to turn it off,
But out popped a rhinoceros.

'Wife!' he shouted loudly,
'Don't turn on any taps.'
But the old lady didn't hear,
Soon the kitchen was full of bats.

The man was so worried,
So do you know what he did?
He went to hide in the toilet,
But in there was a squid.

The old man began to cry out loud,
'My house has turned into a zoo.'
In the attic he could clearly hear
The squawk of an ostrich or two!

On the stairs was an African buffalo,
In the garden was a herd of camels.
Never before had a semi-detached
Been filled with so many mammals.

Amongst the four-legged fiasco,
The man eventually found his wife.
She was fending off a hungry tiger
With a spoon and a butter knife.

He thought about it for a second
And then decided to save himself.
He ran towards the front door,
Passed the rattlesnakes on the shelf.

When he got to his car
The man climbed in and smiled.
What he didn't see in the back
Was a family of crocodiles.

Seasoned

Meal times as slug
Can be quite weird.
Especially when ant spaghetti
Gets stuck in my beard.

Mud soup for breakfast,
A Centipede for tea.
Garnished with grass
And the juice of one flea.

At night I feast on lettuce,
By the light of the moon.
And shelter from the rain
Under the old mushroom.

But now I'm drying up
And I know who's at fault.
It's that mean little boy,
He's just seasoned me with salt.

Gordon

There was a boy called Gordon
Who didn't know how to speak.
Because where his mouth should've been
He had a long and pointy beak.

One day when he was nearly ten,
His friends were sitting down talking.
An interesting thought popped into his head
But he just started squawking.

They all pointed and laughed out loud,
This nearly made Gordon snap.
He went to launch a foul-beaked tirade,
But instead he just said, 'Quack.'

People thought he had no manners,
Gordon never ever said, 'Please.'
He used to spend lunchtime all on his own,
With his face in a packet of seeds.

This beaked-boy kissed his mother once,
It really made her weep.
If you had a son like Gordon,
You'd refuse a peck on the cheek.

Gordon died when he fell from a tree
After singing the dawn chorus.
He landed on his brother, Henry,
Who had tusks just like a walrus.

WoRM

There lived a worm who was quite down to earth,
In fact he was often beneath it.
He'd soil himself on a regular basis
And when he was hungry, he'd eat it.

One day a spade cut the worm in two,
Both halves did a strange little jiggle.
They lay still until the coast was clear
And then they started to wriggle.

The two became the best of friends,
Some said they were even more.
Until the spade came out again,
Then they were a family of four.

Clothes

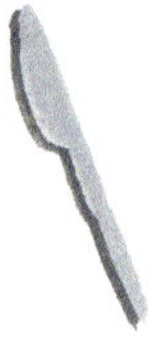

There once was a man
Who liked to eat clothes.
A diet of laundry
Was the one that he chose.

For breakfast he'd eat socks,
For lunch he'd have a shoe.
For supper he'd devour a shirt,
Sometimes he'd have two.

When he was a young boy,
He polished off his dad's slippers.
When his mum told him off,
He scoffed down her knickers.

He once went to the doctors.
'Please help me,' he said.
The doctor soon sent him away
With a prescription for bread.

That didn't help the man,
It only made him worse.
He ate so many dungaree sandwiches,
He very nearly burst.

Insects & Tadpole

'I'm out of here,' shouted Snail,
'I'm going away for good!
I'm bored of never leaving the house!
I want to be a slug!'

'I'm fed up of pollen,' said Bee,
'And I've got hayfever!
Licking flowers isn't a buzz,
I'm too much of a geezer.'

'I'm pulling off my wings,' said Fly,
'Bumping into windows isn't great.
I've seen a really cute beetle
I want to ask her on a date.'

'Carrying heavy things isn't for me,' said Ant,
'My back is starting to hurt a touch.
Get the queen to do some work,
She's a lazy such-and-such!'

'I don't want to be a fly,' cried Maggot,
'I enjoy the ground a lot.
Wriggling is my favourite thing
And I never want to stop!'

'Oh do shut up!' said Tadpole,
'It's not like we have a choice.
I've got a nice big head and a tail,
Soon I'll have four legs and a croaky voice!'

Dinner with a Stork

Smash went the plate,
Clatter went the fork.
This is what happens
When you cook for a stork.

Wings aren't made for cutlery,
Beaks aren't made for glasses.
You couldn't say I was surprised,
By the great amount of smashes.

After dinner the stork crossed his legs.
'Thanks for that,' he said.
'But there was no need for caviar,
I'd have been happier with bread.'

Henry the Shark

Henry had a bit of a problem,
His teeth weren't very sharp.
If he was a giraffe, it wouldn't have been a problem,
But Henry was a shark!

He often looked on jealously
As his friends gobbled up swimmers.
He knew when he got home
It would be seaweed soup for dinner.

When his fin broke through the water,
People would scream in fear.
But when he opened his mouth,
They would only laugh and jeer.

Henry's lowest point came
When he bit into an inflatable seal.
Not even a pop,
Let alone a meal.

Feeling hungry and sad,
The shark began to sing a song.
But he stopped sharply halfway through,
Henry had bitten his tongue!

He did it again just to make sure
And Henry was quite right.
Each one of his little choppers
Was as sharp as a knife.

He quickly swam towards the beach
And jumped out of the water.
Upon realising it was Henry,
People couldn't control their laughter.

A few moments later though,
The laughter had turned to screams.
Henry, he was chortling to himself,
And bursting at the seams.

MR. Snips

As a boy he'd tried jigsaws
And he didn't like sports.
Mr Snips was rather strange,
He liked collecting warts.

He was given his first wart
At the tender age of two.
His dad swiped a pea-sized growth
Off the nose of a kangaroo.

His hobby took him around the world,
Across deserts, mountains and seas.
Wart collecting was an expensive pastime
And never had any guarantees.

Once he travelled to the Amazon,
In search of a rare lump of skin.
In the river was a wart-riddled crocodile,
So Mr Snips jumped right in.

But he should've been more careful,
For crocodiles can be quite ferocious.
When Mr Snips swam back to shore,
He found the outcome quite atrocious.

He didn't get the croc's wart
But he had hundreds of his own.
For the reptile's warts were very contagious,
Mr Snips should've known.

Dreams

'I want to be an astronaut,'
Said Tim to his dad.
'The sky's the limit,' his dad explained,
And that made Tim feel sad.

And Brocco-Lie was a horrible chap,
Not once has he told the truth.
Even when he was caught green-handed,
Chopping off Mrs Parsnip's roots.

Arti-Choke was another mean green,
And yes, he liked to strangle his targets.
That is sadly why in late December,
The leek family didn't make it to market.

Now there wasn't much room in the prison
And not a mushroom either.
For surprisingly these fungal growths
Were high academic achievers.

Back at the over-crowded prison,
Things were fast turning quite rotten.
A cell block full of murderous potatoes
Had been completely forgotten.

The decaying spuds were beginning to stink
And the other prisoners weren't at all pleased.
A gang of carrots in the cell next door
Were worried about becoming diseased.

A riot soon began all over the prison,
The sight was quite distressing.
Especially when in cell number six,
An old cauliflower started undressing.

When the peas escaped and started a fire,
The flames spread quicker than ever.
And we all know that veg shouldn't be burnt,
But the peas weren't very clever.

The prisoner chards screamed.
'Everyone out!' They yelled.
Soon the bad tempered veg
Were free from their cells.

Instead behaving themselves,
The mean vegetables turned savage.
They kicked the heads off flowers
And Beat-Root killed a cabbage.

The top of the garden
Looked like a battle scene.
You could smell burning veg for miles
And the paving stones were stained green.

The chaos eventually came to an end,
Soon after a flock of starlings landed on the fence.
'I would tuck right in,' said one bird to another,
'But at the moment things look tense.'

A courageous starling chirped,
'I know it looks quite risky.
But I'm going to have my lunch now,
Before those greens get too crispy.'

A White-Tailed John Called Moose

There was a beaver,
A beaver called Steve.
That people used to call Beave,
The beaver called Steve.

So the stever called Beave.
I mean beaver called Steve,
Was very aggrieved
And rather quite peeved.

Beave couldn't believe
That people called him Steve.
Actually that's wrong,
I mixed up Steve and Beave.

One day Steve was playing
With his friend called Matt.
You'll be delighted to know,
Matt was a rat.

They wanted someone else to play with,
So they found their friend Tyson.
You'll be pleased to know,
Tyson was a bison.

They wanted someone else to join in,
So they called on their friend Bruce.
You'll be happy to know,
Bruce was a moose.

They wanted someone else to play with,
So they visited their friend John.
You'll be surprised to know,
John was a white-tailed deer.

So Beave and Rat,
And Bison and Bruce.
Actually, that's wrong,
I meant Bruce not moose.

I did actually mean Bruce,
The name I got wrong was Bison.
And Beave too.
But John's a white-tailed Matt called Tyson.

So once and for all,
I'll go through it again.
Because remembering all these names
Can be quite a pain.

Beaver's a Steve called Deer,
Rat's a Matt called Moose.
Tail's a white deer called John,
And don't forget the bison called Bruce.

So the white-tailed John called Moose,
And the Matt called Beave,
And the Tyson called Bison,
Played with a deer called Steve.

Chips

Chip Stealer was his name
And chip stealing was his game.
He stole chips from the ends of forks
And for his crimes he found fame.

He'd wait on the harbour wall
For his chance to swoop.
But if people had them wrapped not open,
He'd fly over them and poop.

People used to come for miles
To watch this thief in motion.
He was the most famous bird
This side of the Atlantic Ocean.

At last came his chance to steal
A chip from an old crooked man.
The old man stuck his fork in a chip,
He was about to eat it then... WHAM!

What happened next was not very nice
But every gull has his day.
Chip Stealer has swallowed the fork
And he was about to pay.

He spluttered and coughed
But the fork was stuck.
Old Chip Stealer,
He'd ran out of luck.

The old crooked man,
He laughed and quipped.
'Look at that fat seagull,
He's had his chips!'

Eight Hands

Being an octopus can be quite handy,
Especially when preparing food.
Slicing and dicing and mixing and whisking,
Can be done while the dog gets shampooed.

The washing can be hung out
Whilst all the beds are made.
And the windows can be cleaned
When at the same time Scrabble is played.

One young octopus was very smug
About his talented tentacles.
One day when he was in the bath,
He stole the neighbour's vegetables.

Rather than use his legs for good,
The octopus committed offences.
Once he was playing cards with himself
When pulled down he neighbours fences.

This made the octopus laugh out loud
But made the man next door furious.
Mr Smith only had two arms
But the plan he hatched was glorious.

Mr Smith was a small old man
But his brain was a fair old size.
The octopus may have had eight legs
But he wasn't very wise.

When the octopus was sleeping,
The man snuck into his house.
And whilst he set up his chainsaw,
The man was as quiet as a mouse.

When he fired it up though,
The noise caused such a commotion.
The octopus woke up with a shock
And wished he'd stayed in the ocean.

Mr Smith was frothing at the mouth,
He wasn't going to be nice.
He intended to get his revenge,
Leg by leg and slice by slice.

Yummy

He'd put a spoon of gunpowder in his tea
So that his farts would explode.
They'd be followed by a wisp of smoke
That could be seen from across the road.

He'd eat battery sandwiches for lunch,
To help him stay awake for longer.
And although he didn't tell anyone this,
He did it to make himself stronger.

He'd eat a pickled elastic band
If his back was a little stiff.
It never made him more flexible,
But the man used to insist.

His weird and wonderful remedies,
They really were a fascinating thing.
He gargled with vinegar for seventeen weeks,
In an attempt to help him sing.

It had the opposite effect though,
The strange man lost his voice.
He eventually got it back on Tuesday night,
After eating a meal of songbird feathers and rice.

And what a voice it was,
The songbird feathers really did the trick.
It wasn't long before he was top of the charts,
But then he suddenly fell sick.

He was too ill to treat himself
And the doctors didn't know what to do.
They were just about to give up
When the man began to spew.

First out came fourteen batteries,
Followed by elastic bands and rice.
Then came some feathers and vinegar,
The sight of this wasn't very nice.

The man however was as good as new
And he leapt up out of the bed!
'I feel very hungry!' he shouted.
'I'll mop this mess up with some bread!'

Animal Noises

SQUEAK!

'Shush, shush, shush!'
Said the rat to the cat.
'What's with all this meowing?'

'Buzz, buzz, buzz!'
Said the bee to the flea.
'Stop bouncing or I'll sting you.'

'Ribbit, ribbit, ribbit!'
Said the frog to the dog.
'Your barking is scaring my tadpole.'

'Grunt, grunt, grunt!'
Said the bull to the gull.
'Please don't drop chips on my head.'

'Roar, roar, roar!'
Said the tiger to the spider.
'Your spindly legs really scare me!'

'Squeak, squeak, squeak!'
Said the vole to mole.
'Why are you always digging?'

'Meow, meow, meow!'
Said the cat to the rat.
'I'll make all the noise I want to!'

'Ha ha ha!'
Said the flea to the bee.
'You'll have to catch me first!'

'Woof, woof, woof!'
Said the dog to the frog.
'I'll have your tadpole for dinner!'

'Squawk, squawk, squawk!'
Said the gull to the bull.
'Because you said please I'll only drop peas!'

'Oh, oh, oh!'
Said the spider to the tiger.
'Your teeth aren't too friendly either!'

'Snort, snort, snort!'
Said the mole to vole.
'Why are you asking me questions?'

Frog

'Meow,' said the cat.
'Woof,' said the dog.
'Je ne comprends pas,'
Said a sophisticated frog.

You see this little amphibian
Was not your typical pond dweller.
He'd spend many days and nights
Tasting the wine in his cellar.

He preferred to dine out in fine restaurants
Rather than catch flies.
And had an unhealthy obsession
With his collection of bowties.

One day he was at a restaurant,
When to the waiter he said, 'What's new?'
The man led the frog to the kitchen
And threw him in a stew!

'Don't cook me!' he croaked,
But I'm afraid it was too late.
Minutes later his legs were being chewed
By a young couple on a date.

Said the man to his lover,
"This really is quite fine.
I keep getting the slightest hint
Of some very good red wine."

Animal Olympics

The Animal Olympics
Is a sight to behold,
Where else will a cheetah
Fairly win gold?

The high diving crocodiles
Is an amazing spectacle,
And watching octopus kung fu
Is quite exceptional.

Four-legs, feathers, beaks,
Scales and bills,
Creatures travel from all over
To show off their skills.

Synchronized swimming
Is always won by the seals.
Whilst watching the sloth 10,000 meters,
Can be quite an ordeal.

Geese competing in archery
Is often worth a gander,
When a goose was accidently skewered
The event ended in slander.

High jumping kangaroos
Are always reaching new heights.
Whilst watching the hippopotamus pentathlon,
Is quite a delight.

But my favourite event to watch,
Despite all these great games,
Is watching the snakes cook the spectator's burgers,
Last year one ended up in flames.

Girl with a Moustache

She'd brush it before school,
She'd brush it before bed.
"Please stop brushing it,"
Her mum and dad said.

She cared for it more
Than the hair on her head.
To her this monstrosity
Was the best thing since sliced bread.

She'd had it when she was born
And loved it ever since.
Despite the fact it was very spiky,
And made her grandparents wince.

"I'll never shave it off!"
Said the girl to her friend.
Would her love for this eyesore
Ever see an end?

Her eccentric look
Became the talk of the town.
The fuss about her fuzz
Refused to die down.

Reluctant though they were,
Her parents took her to a 'facial furniture' competition.
They even bought her wax
To help the ends of it glisten.

There wasn't any argument
When the girl was awarded first prize.
It was a magnificent moustache,
What pleased the judges was the size.

And I'm not being presumptuous,
The size would've impressed you too.
One end of her moustache was in London
The other was in Timbuktu.

About the Author

Carl Stefan Wiezak is a relatively normal man. He likes to have a bath and is father to twin-pests, Jessica and May. When not being a dad, he can be found gardening, walking, running, listening to music, checking the weather and daydreaming.